To The Far Country

new poems by
June Sidran Mandelkern

Tall Trees Press
West Hartford CT

To The Far Country

Tall Trees Press
West Hartford, CT 06117

jsmandelkern@gmail.com

ISBN: 978-0-692-03184-1

Front & back cover photographs: Kathy Strauss | ImageWerks | www.imagewerks.net

Internal Photographs by June Sidran Mandelkern

For my grandchildren:
Talya, Carmi, Ronit, Neal and Nora Mandelkern

Contents

IV // Sorrow And Loss 55

V // Renewal 71

Acknowledgments

Many people have contributed to the successful publication of this book. Special thanks to:

My son Nick Mandelkern who is a constant source of strength and support; my sister Sonya Greenfield who is my oldest and truest confidant; my sons Michael and Peter Mandelkern for their steadfast presence in my life; my friend Adlyn Loewenthal for the long afternoons of editorial assistance and advice to move the book forward; Joe Keeney, book shepherd extraordinaire, who packaged it and made it happen; Kathy Strauss whose consummate artistry produced the front and back cover photographs and made it come alive; Cantor Pamela Siskin who stands by me in good times and bad and whose well of lovingkindness is inexhaustible; librarian Marcia Lewis who provided the nurturing environment for these poems to grow; the Faxon Poets who were the first to hear them; Tom Nicotera, gentle poet mentor; and Steve Olechna, editor of the Faxon Poets' yearly anthologies, *Perspectives I–X,* 2006-2016, in which many of these poems were first printed.

Thanks also to my friends Marilyn Hott, Enid Rothenberg, Beverly Lavender, Martha Clancy, Estelle Dansky, Mairead Lazarus and Sharon Cormier, who stand beside me with help and encouragement; and finally to the memory of my deceased husband Robert Mandelkern whose sixty years of devotion provided the backup and inspiration for all of this work.

I
NATURE'S REALM

Antarctica 1996

Butterfly Bush

My friends gave me a butterfly bush,
the kind that brings transcendent beings
to their verdant garden all summer.
Diminutive bodies with bright wings
light timorously on luminous flowers
to delight the eye of the lucky watcher.

Every child knows the story, the journey
from larvae to pupa in cocoons of their own
design to burst forth in glowing splendor.
We have heard of miraculous flights
to their winter home where Monarch butterflies
cover earth and trees as a blanket of living color.

Lovingly I planted my small bush.
Compassionate chipmunks allowed it to thrive
as it grew to window height with purple flowers
blooming in quiet joy.

Alas! Although I live on the edge of woods,
wetlands not to be destroyed, where wildlife flourishes
and stately deer emerge, birds dart vividly as flocks
of crows descend in fluid group dynamics,
in vain I waited for my butterflies.

I cut back my bush for winter snows
till spring will bring it forth again.
As we said in the Brooklyn of my childhood
when the Dodgers played in Ebbets Field:
wait till next year!
You gotta believe, and I do.

Power

On my azalea bush
woven between the leaves
a spider's web glistens
in the morning light
with pearls of water.

Why have I been given such power
to destroy it with one sweep
of my broom
or let it live
in beauty one more day?

Fantasia

Bare branches in the upper canopy
sway with simple grace
stand unbreachable
by massed clouds
poised to engulf us

myself at the trees
imagine a silken cord
attached at the top of my head
gently pulls me upward
away from rooted earth

linger a moment at the summit
swiftly part the clouds
leap with giant stride
to perch on the outer rim

sit relaxed and free
in eternal radiant sunlight

to open my throat
to find my voice
and sing

Rhododendron

after the rainy spring
flowering plants
bloom everywhere

blossoms on my front lawn
halfway up the window
in shades of lilac
hint of pink within

these surpass them all
greeting me riotously
in joyful release
from winter snow

Winter Beach

To see the beach in winter
is to know it whole.

Vacationers' delight no longer,
unclothed in shades of gray,
skeletal bones protrude
gaunt and spare.

Seabirds own the shore,
soar and dip in elemental dance.

The lone watcher feels the surge,
primitive and everlasting
yet eternal symbol of change,
merging light and shadow,
land and sea as one.

Rainbow of Hope

A rainbow appeared this morning
in my shower stall
sliding under the window shade
around the curtain's edge,

red and orange streaks of light
glowing on the seat
of the white shower chair,
reflected on the floor.

My breath caught in stunned delight
as shards of color pierced despair,
mute companion of old age,
with power to quiet suffering,

reminding us again that courage,
hope and beauty, though
obscured by pain and sadness,
can still illuminate our lives.

Mopsie

alpha dog in miniature frame
bosses the squirrels high
in the trees
with excited canine chatter

moist button nose in
soft white fur
with eyes that mirror
her soul

how she wishes
she could talk

and so indeed
do we

Canine Love

The big brown dog on a long leash
held in the hand of a teenage boy
dutifully follows his master.

Somewhere in his evolutionary memory
he was a strong wild creature
cousin to the wolf, hunting
in packs untamed and free.

What road led him
to this subservient fate,
domesticated by the hand of man
to serve as household pet,
humanity's best friend and pal?

Under the benign persona
does a vestige of the feral brain remain?
Does he long to find again that
lost and savage wildness in his soul?

Home to supper and the children
once again.

Fabric of Time

I set the timer
for a three-minute egg
and I walk away.

If I sit and watch it
will the passage of time
be any more real?

Sea of Cortez

skimming over the Mexican sea
toward the rocky island
where sea lions mate

nursing babies cling to mothers
massive males rest together
barking raucous cries

spray from the small boat glistens
in rays of a late-day sun
glancing off the shores

    I long to remember
    in the cold dark days ahead

the breeze impossibly gentle
waters transparently clear
powerful mammals at home
on the rise of their low brown hills

remember this bountiful pageant
oasis alive in the sunlight
one moment of peace and joy

August Lament

Deep greens laced with gold
portend the end of summer.
I am not ready yet for fall.

I am not ready yet for bitter wind
in place of easy breeze,
for woolen scarves and heavy shoes.
My heart still yearns to keep
the simple pace of summer,
lengthened days, quiet breaths,
senses slowed and drawing in.

A chipmunk smaller than my hand
sits motionless, alert
upon my garden table.
If I just make a sound
it will vanish like
the summer winding down.

Will my garden table still
be here next year, and I
to watch another vibrant soul
in fullness of its life,

and will the summer air
move softly through the leaves
to bring this tender melancholy
home to me again?

II
ON BEING HUMAN

McKee Springs, Utah 1998

On Being Human

Ultimately we live each one alone.
Although we are placenta born
from birth in need of nurture
tied to the clan with bonds of steel
since first we roamed the grassy plains--

although all blood runs red
it is enclosed within one bioframe
with certain death if it leaks out
to mingle freely.
Ultimately we stand each one alone.

In the time it takes the earth
to turn ten times around the sun,
in that real time perhaps
I shall be here no more.

I do not regret the loss of DNA
so much of which we share
with all life forms since time began:
it is the loss of consciousness I mourn,
unique, unshared and singular,
until that moment unforeseen as yet
when my small footprints shall be
covered by the sands.

Ultimately we stand and fall alone,
this is our glory and our pain.

The Alien

An alien being dwells within my skin.
Where is she who should be living here?

In some distant island dawn perhaps
she greets the mountain jagged
at the water's edge, feels the sea spray
bite the air, walks the beach
to gather shells to place upon her table
with her solitary breakfast.

As she drinks her morning tea
her kitchen window reveals a meadow
opulent and wide, redolent with flowers,
vibrant color marching to the hills,
bird sounds and muted hum of life.

In such an alternate world
there would be time to catch
the vagrant thoughts that flutter past,
gather in and hold them close
before they vanish to the void,

time to recognize the inner strivings
longing to be heard, to sing
the unsung songs and savor peace
in quiet harmony.

While I, the alien and I,
are caught in duty's piercing glare
irresolute, immobilized and mute.

Mounted

I ride a bucking steed
spirited and difficult to hold
        with balance

climbing steeply to the hills
deeply plunging in the valleys
snorting at the wind that rushes past
        with terrifying speed

        I long to dismount
        to a green meadow
        gentle with flowers

and when at last I do
when the ride is over
when the spent mount
stands quivering at my side

when my trembling limbs
touch solid earth again
        what then?

Swimmer

in waters dark and still I swim
remote from land
abyss below in silence absolute
automaton limbs
move rhythmically
reflexive stroke by stroke

    not respite nor succor
    is on the horizon
    no harbor safe in view

the goal is in the journey
ever onward
forward to an unseen shore

Quest

Drop by drop the water
wears away the stone
as the high peak reverts to level plain.
So the minutes of my life scroll by
squandering my allotted heart beats
in dutiful tedium.

Somewhere in the distance stands
the mountain I have yet to climb,

somewhere the broad wings
to fly me through the night sky
streaked with shards of red and gold
toward the rising sun,

somewhere the stout boat to ferry me
to sunlit islands blessed with peace,

somewhere the quiet road edged
with flowers leading to a meadow
serene and calm where time is slowed
and truth can be allowed to speak.

No one will come to rescue me.
My knight is likely in a nursing home
his walker by his side,
TV remote in hand.

Only I can hear my plea,
I am both seeker and finder.
The quest is mine alone.
The answer lies within,
in patience waiting for my call.

Supernova

The atoms in our bodies were forged
in the throes of dying stars many light years
from the small rock we call our home.
We are the refuse of this stellar system
whirling through infinity of space.

Life-sustaining water, oxygen we burn
for fuel, amino acids in our tissues,
all accidental debris, by-products
of an ever-changing cosmos hurtling
at unimaginable speed to its unknown destiny.

Does time, created in the cataclysm
whimsically called the Big Bang,
have only one direction, any purpose?
We cling to our island sphere
barely a footnote to the grandeur
around us, ever closer to that moment
when our earth will be consumed
in fire from its exhausted sun.

Whether sentient beings will be there
as watchers we can only speculate.
Did dinosaurs or Neanderthals
contemplate their own demise?

Let those minds able to deal
with such abstractions work
their mathematical equations,
search for fleeting unknown particles
to solve the riddles of the universe.

We toilers in the fields below
can but experience the majesty
and heartbreak of this moving,
morphing speck of comfort on which
we spend our brief and fragile lives.

If a star explodes in the firmament
and no one is there as witness:

What is the true reality?

Defiance

I paint purple polish on my toes.

As our beloved planet
dangles in the void
disasters poise to strike at random:

seismic eruptions without warning,
burning lava hissing to the sea,
communities drown in tsunamis' wake,
children die as schools collapse,

hunger and disease sweep rampant,
communities homeless and displaced,
women abused, discarded like rag dolls,

bells daily toll for human life
in every quarter of the globe.

But I shall pursue
my own small act of defiance
to keep my purple polish
shining on my toes.

Searching and Seeking

Searching and seeking,
longing for the whole:

I want to gulp the days,
to shout and hear my voice,
to pierce my heart with joy.

I want
to grasp the hugeness of the universe,
to breathe the many colors of the air,
to see triangles morph into the square,
the circle molded to the sphere.

I want
to pluck the overhanging fruit,
spit out the seeds to grow again
for future lives to share.

And when I fall
I want to be accepting of my fate,
and know that I have sought my truth
alone and unafraid.

Creativity

My cousin Eve put glorious paint to canvas,
pictures that excite the quiet walls.
One day she set down her brushes
and never picked them up again.
    If I had such talent
    I would never let it go.
My sister Miriam studied data
from satellites to earth.
When she retired from university
she stopped doing physics.
    If I had such knowledge
    I would never let it go.

And now I find
my words have flown away.
I think of them as endless flocks of birds
limitless as the value of pi
congregating in space huddled
with words stored in the cloud
or languishing in unread books
waiting to be recalled like orphans
longing to be chosen.

Is it my fault they have left me?
Have I been lazy, too busy
with daily duties, too engrossed
in the struggle for survival
to keep them safe at home?

If I quiet my mind to absolute zero
will the vacuum draw them back again?
    I will never let them go.

Gazelles

my words begin to form
in my brain fresh from sleep
before I am fully awake

they dance into my mind like gazelles
moving across my consciousness
not shy but fleeting if

I don't catch them at once
transfer them to solid matter
with pen and paper

they are so beautiful
in their unrealized state
I wish I did not have to capture

fence them in to lose
their gossamer form
to corporeal reality

but oh how lovely it is
that they still come to me
they have not yet left me

for more fertile fields
they assemble in the wings
to appear again at dawn

in their celestial orbit
across the hopeful palette
of my mind

Nomenclature

My grandchildren call me Junie
and I love it.

When they were small my husband,
their grandfather, and I
referred to ourselves as Junie and Bobby.
The names held, and we loved it.

When we came to pick them up
at nursery school
all the children would chant
"Junie and Bobby are here".
And we loved it.

Their parents thought it disrespectful:
We thought it the ultimate of respect.

Over the years I've tried
to persuade my sons to call me
by my name to no avail:
they persist in calling me Mom.

Don't get me wrong,
I heartily approve of Moms.
It is good to be Mom,
but I think June or Junie
would be fine.

There are many Moms out there
but only one me, their Mom,
unique and individual,
June or Junie.
I would love it indeed.

Wisdom

When I was eighteen
I didn't have a clue
what life was all about.

Many decades later
I've taken all the punches
fate has thrown at me – and now

reeling but still standing
gamely waiting for the bell,
experienced and wiser:

I still don't have a clue.

III
TO THE FAR COUNTRY

Thingvellir National Park, Iceland 2004

The Far Country

I have crossed into the country of old age.
The barrier was down,
        unknowing I wandered in.
No signs were at the outpost,
        no warnings to observe.

Here is the sign I would post:

—Before you enter here

        Strengthen your inner defenses
        Determine your own reality
        Develop a true identity and hold it fast

As heat and pressure assault you
do not become sedimentary
bits and pieces of your former self
        easily eroded

but harden to crystalline clarity,
micaceous sheen reflective
        of your seminal truth.

In the country of the very old
these are the things that sustain us:
        hand of a friend,
        voice of a child,
        mind resilient and engaged,

to be part of the order of things
        when we want it,
or step out of the line
        if we choose.

Dichotomy

I am an old woman.
In a third world country I would have
no teeth. I might be found sitting
on the pavement with a grandchild
on my lap smiling my toothless grin.

Lucky am I to have expensive dentistry,
corrective surgery for my eyes, funds
and leisure for the gym. Lucky am I
with clean water and indoor plumbing,
house warm in winter, cool in summer,
newspapers, television and internet
to connect me with the world.

Why then do I feel this strange dichotomy,
an odd affinity with the toothless crone?
Would I trade my teeth for a place
at her table, to know that heavy work is left
to younger, stronger backs? Would I trade
my place in this affluent society for surety
that willing hands will lift me
when I can no longer walk
and only loving voices call my name?

When the time comes to abandon
independence this is the price we pay:
left to the care of underpaid workers
in the nursing home, or to live in isolation
prey to loneliness and despair.

Indeed, I am one of the lucky ones.
Or am I lucky indeed?

Generations

I dreamed I met my mother,
pink-cheeked, white hair and frail,
at a restaurant with friends
seated at a table on the patio
sheltered by a striped umbrella,

myself the incarnation
of the fifty year old daughter
who traveled from suburbia to Brooklyn
for the weekly ritual lunch.

Just before her eighty-seventh birthday
her heart failed her at last
(seemingly to me so old!)
Now in my late decades
I see the dual aspects of myself,
generations molded to each other.

In the dream she did not speak
as I bantered with her friends,
her face suffused with pleasure
at my presence, emotion
understood by all that lingered
when the dream dissolved.

It takes such little effort
to give comfort to the old,
never fully realized
until the dream is gone.

Lineage

Exiled from home with my ailing husband
by a late October storm that thrust
thick wet snowflakes on towering trees
still heavy with autumn leaves
to bring down power lines and blanket
the northeast in early cold and darkness

I visit my son in a New England town
on the Connecticut shore, thankful
to have found haven, generous, kind and safe.

On a crisp November day I walk up the hill
to an old cemetery surrounded by
a high stone wall, graves of colonists
dating back two hundred years or more.
Those buried here are gone much longer
than they lived, their footsteps long erased.

Abandoned and forlorn the limestone markers
stand, some upright still, some tilted
toward the earth, incised words blurred
by wind and weather, or undecipherable.
On the ground I find two headstones,
legends clear:

Esther
Wife of
Gershon Bulkely
Daughter of
Samuel Morehouse
Died
Jan. 24, 1871
Aged 82 years
& 10 mo's

The other reads, more economically

Gershon Bulkeley
Died
June 23, 1830
Aged 46 years
& 6 mo's

Both stones broken from their base lie
side by side united in eternity of death.

In gentle melancholy now I speak to her.
Esther, my comrade, my sister,
could you have been my friend?
Would we have spent time drinking tea
together, exchanging recipes and gossip,
discussing politics, domestic and beyond?

Were you literate, could you read books
and poems, or write perhaps like me?
Was your marriage happy, your husband kind?
Many years a widow, did you support yourself
or look to others for sustenance,
object of charity and pity?.

Oh Esther, my sister, my friend,
would that many children graced
your widowhood, helped you
cross the line dividing life and death
to ease your pain and comfort you.
Somewhat I envy you, your final certitude,
your life fulfilled, your journey done.

I stroll back down the hill at peace, returned
to warmth and safety, to my own reality.
Some day will someone sit upon my grave
and softly speak to me
and whisper words like these?

How long, perhaps, how soon?

Twilight

I linger on the streets of life
unsure of my direction,
if indeed there is direction.

Perhaps this is my destination.
Perhaps there is no resolution,
perhaps this is where I must be.

Muted grayness coats the land,
all sign posts vanished,
warmth and joy are fled.
The road is long and I am tired.

Where is the hearth I have been seeking,
where the outstretched arm
to keep me from a stumble,
the quiet peace at journey's end?

Dusk descends,
the night is falling fast
and I know not where I am.

Tiger at the Gate

The tiger paces at the gate,
teeth bared, hungry to attack,
waiting for the moment,
knowing it will come.

We are but prey.
Safe within the walls
we breathe and soldier on,
waiting for the moment,
knowing it will come.

November

November has overtaken my soul:
beauty and terror locked in combat,
no doubt about the outcome.

Trees are bare with foreboding,
night comes earlier each day.
Loneliness seeps through chinks
in the doors, storms
gather their forces in distant seas.
Warmth from the sun is a memory
from happier times.

It is a long way till Spring,
a myth retold in firelight.
Summer is as distant
as the cold and barren moon.

The earth closes in on itself
and hunkers down; the spirit
longs for return of light
hoping it can come in time.

Arrow of Time

Walking hand in hand into the sunset
is a pipe dream invented by an ad man.
We in the twilight of our lives
know the bitter reality.

When I was fifty and my mother
came to my suburban home to sleep
in the guest room over the garage,
she said the room was cold.
I thought: she is ungrateful!

Today I know the room was cold
over the unheated garage,
her older bones more sensitive.
Mother, can you hear me?
Mother, I can hear you now!

This is the end of the fantasy.
Reflexes slow, the body aches,
rainbows fade, the sunsets dull.

We cling to each other for comfort
as the arrow of time points forward
inexorably moving on.

On The Road

The path of old age has many hazards
looming in the shadows: falls,
infections, joint and muscle pains,
and those great sappers of the will,
anxiety and depression.

The struggle is ongoing,
a treadmill slowly moving in reverse.
As outer strength wanes, inner strength
becomes the only mantra.

Though the ascent may be steep
and the road beyond the bend
hidden in obscurity, willing hands
and laughter shared can ease
the steps along the way.

Canyon Ranch

Shadows of the past flicker in the corners
recalling days when we could run
and jump and stretch, lie on the floor
and never give a thought to getting up again.

Young couples, echo of our former selves,
cannot imagine time when exercise machines
stress aging joints, muscle cramps appear
at will, tennis is a sport for watching
and the pool too cold for comfort.

Beauty of the Berkshire hills surrounds us still,
tinged with nostalgia and loss. My love,
the days of strength and vigor are behind us,
managing our frailties is the option at hand.

Long hallways once traversed with ease
present a challenge now, youthful kindness
of the staff appears in gentle mockery

Perhaps this is the last time I will walk
these memoried halls, inhale
the fragrant warmth of wood-burning fire
in contrast to the gleam of snow
outside the tall transparent windows.

Perhaps it will be best to leave the ghosts
behind, to let the incarnation
of our younger selves vanish
with the smoke into the air,
as we pull our tattered courage close
around our shoulders in a world
we never dreamed could ever come.

Caregiver

Today my name is Atlas,
heavy on my shoulders sits the world.
Why was I thus ordained to be
the CEO of everything, keeper of the flame?

It used to be you who instigated meetings
with lawyers and financial advisers
as I dutifully agreed to all decisions,
uncritical and unfocused.
You were the mover and shaker
firmly in control of our future,
so far off, so little heeded…
the future, suddenly arrived.

Now you, laden with infirmities of age
and crippled with progressive disease,
alternate between awareness and sleep,
your mind hobbled with medications and pain.
Your life is now a butterfly
lightly resting on my hands.

Dear butterfly, I cannot always
keep you safe from predators and storms.
In this brief moment of calm
I lift my hands in pleading to the universe:

Grant us once more, for however short a time,
the power to breathe unrestricted by fate,
to savor again in dual harmony
the old melodic rhythm of our lives
before it flies from us forever.

The Brave Ones

The country of old age
is not for faint of heart.
Guideposts are gone, each

wanders his own field
daily to reinvent the wheel.
New paths are forged,

burdens of the past carried
toward a future wrapped in fog
mined with unknown fears.

Our children cannot save us,
they live in their own dimension.

We smile, invite each other
to lunch, return to our quiet
homes to count our blessings

while deep in the shadows
the monsters wait,
the wild things still out there.

We cry to the wilderness,
hear our call! Behold!
Notice us, see us!
We are the warriors,

we are the brave ones
who stumble through the night
defenseless and unarmed
toward a dawn
that may never come.

IV
SORROW AND LOSS

Redwoods National Park, Orick CA 1992

Cindy

your brightness stilled
your fluent wit
your ready laugh
your quick bird movements
hovering from task to task
all gone

heavy and slowed in your last two years
from the poisons they fed you
even then your grace came shining through
your active teacher's mind
extending in concentric circles
touching all around you
especially the children

always the children…

your brightness stilled
your grace shot down
your flight suspended in mid-air

Cindy 2

Your children keep your picture
near their pillows,
your voice and face receding
in the mist,
your projects with them
never to be finished,
no new ones ever to be done.

Other hands must move them forward,
other voices call their names.
You, who fought the odds to bear them,
death has torn you from their grasp.

Your husband's grief obscures
his lonely vision.
The path ahead is shrouded
in his pain.

Wearily,
 bewildered and abandoned,
the survivors lift their packs
and stumble on.

Cindy 3

On the second Mother's Day
after your death
your husband took your children
to the beach
because you loved the beach
to gather shells
and small smooth stones
to place upon your grave.

Your elder daughter chose
a potted plant of tall white roses
and set it carefully
surrounded by the shells
and stones
wordlessly to affirm
their love and longing.

Another year
has moved your children forward
into early adolescence
into middle childhood
leaving you behind
alone
forever young.

The cemetery is not
a place to visit
on Mother's Day
but it is all we have.

Cindy 4

tall in the August sun
your tombstone palely gleams
pink marble polished
delicately curved at the top

deep clear inscription
WIFE MOTHER DAUGHTER
SISTER TEACHER FRIEND
your children's names in Hebrew letters

in the center firmly fastened
a heart of pure white marble
the single word MOM

flowers planted by your friends
surround the base
your children place their offerings
of shells and stones
to keep you company

years have passed since we brought you here
still unacceptably unbelievably
unaccountably true

muted sadness has replaced despair
other struggles now engage us
other faces float in front of yours

we cannot allow the dead to win
it would defeat us all
including you

Anniversary

anniversary
of your death

in early morning freshness
we mourn you

in strident heat of noon
we grieve

you cannot hear
        your children
cannot see them
        grow

in pallid evening
gray dust settles
as we mourn you
as we grieve

to the rising dawn
we turn our faces

tenderly
        reluctantly
we give you back
        to time
        again

Edith

your life's work left unfinished
        uncharacteristic of you

the competent one who knew the answers
        or combed the internet to find them

who gloried in your children and grandchildren
        now shorn of your sheltering wing

who patiently handled your taciturn husband
        protective cover now torn away

who joyfully shopped for bargains
        matching outfits and shoes
returned from Costco with supplies
        for your overfilled cupboards

you left, abandoned it all

the mirror you searched for perfectly framed
        hangs yet over the couch
tiles in the foyer carefully chosen
        lie still under our feet
earrings you made for my birthday
        remain in my jewelry box

treasures of your history
left as we are left
bereft of your comforting presence

forsaken in one brief moment
forsaken and left behind

Edith's Tree

the tree in your front yard
barely higher than a tall man
graced by early blooms of April
white flowers on slender stalks
heralds spring's recurrent theme
vibrant life unfolding
new again

another year you are not here
to see the petals glowing in the light
to feel the breeze awaken them
to watch them lightly dancing on the air

fragile blossoms soon to lie
damply on the earth

while I am left to mourn
the memory of my friend who
unlike the tremulous flowers
will not return to bloom again
in spring

Island Sands

Once
we walked barefoot
on island sands
fingers linked,
laughed in the sunset,
drank our toasts and knew
that it would last forever.

Now
I stand alone
upon an alien shore
shivering in bitter winds
exposed to the onrushing storm,
your hand no longer safe
in mine, your voice
forever silent in the night.

Where has it gone, our island?
Where did it go, the dream?

Valentine's Day

On Valentine's Day
a few days before your death
I brought to you, home-bound
in the isolation of illness and old age,
a small heart-shaped box of candy,
and one for your caregiver too.

Many years ago in the early years
of our marriage you gave to me
on Valentine's Day an elegant
Coach shoulder-strap handbag.
Tan leather, utterly simple in design,
it took my breath away.

Enjoyed for many seasons it was
at last donated to a thrift shop.
I like to think it still hangs on the door
of some old woman's closet.

If I had it now, worn, creased
and shabby with use, I would cry
perhaps, not for the expensive gift
given in an extravagant gesture
by a fond young husband,

but for the small box of candy
bought in a chain drug store
shortly before you left me.

This year on Valentine's Day
I shall buy myself a crimson
heart-shaped box of candy
and against all medical and dental

protocol I shall savor every piece,
as I light your memorial candle
and take comfort in the flickering glow
of its warm and steady flame.

Artifacts

The toy monkey grins at me
from its perch on the headboard of my bed.
Improbably pink, bought for a visit
to a toddler that never occurred,
it joined the cheerful group
of small stuffed animals that comfort me
each night since you are gone.

Here is the brown moose with tan antlers
from the hotel shop in Vermont
where we celebrated our fifty-fifth aniversary
when you, already unable to walk
to restaurants and shops in town,
were shepherded by car the few steps required.

Here is the sturdy buffalo, symbol
of the American spirit, wild prairie grasses
and open plains, I bought for you in Wyoming
on a trip you were not able to join.

Here is the sad-faced dog given to you
by a friend after one of your hospital stays
resting its chin on the worn fabric, floppy ears
dangling and short black tail bravely aloft,

and here is the white bear with blue
Jewish stars on the soles of its feet and
a "Happy Hanukkah" sign across the chest
brought to our door by kind members
of our synagogue during your long last illness.

Above is the three-dimensional dream-catcher
with twelve strands of turquoise ribbons
purchased long ago at the gift shop
of an indigenous tribe on the Olympic Peninsula,
when time had no meaning and the future
stretched before us unending and free.

Artifacts of our story, I honor them
as they soldier on, require no sustenance
but the blessing of memory, which happily
has not yet been taken from me.

Thank You For Your Service

On the wall behind my bed
hangs a cap with the words
"World War II Veteran" embroidered
on it. I cannot bear to part with it.

In 1942 at the age of seventeen
he enlisted in the Navy to fight
in what we called the last good war.

The few remaining veterans
of that terrible conflict are dying
at a daily rate. They are called
the greatest generation, and perhaps
they were, although I must have hope
for the future.

When he wore the cap people would say,
thank you for your service.
Now that he is gone sometimes
I find myself talking to it.

Thank you for your service, I say,
thank you for surviving the brutal war,
thank you for sharing my life,
thank you for sixty years of family,
thank you for your unwavering devotion
even as your body faltered and faded.

Thank you,
Thank you for your service.

Grief

After you died, I suddenly grew old.

Together we were living your last years
in full intensity, crisis after crisis,
alert to your comfort and freedom
from pain. Home bound,
confined to a small arena,
all foods were chosen to please you,
television shows and sports events,
all visitors invited for your interest.

Until, on an ordinary Friday morning
no different from any other in February
your life began to wane
and one day later you were gone.
In memory those hours are blurred,
I stood like the paper dolls of my childhood
propped up by wings of cardboard,
following protocol and tradition
obediently.

Now the winter is upon us again,
the chill creeps back and painfully
I am aware you are not here.
But I have grown old – so old,
vulnerable to the winds of fate,
my cardboard wings collapsing
in the icy rain.

I understand your voice is gone.
How can I keep from losing mine?

V
RENEWAL

Oregon Dunes National Momument, 1994

Carousel

The carousel of life spins fitfully.
I fear I have overstayed my welcome.

Attendants are long gone,
my ticket of admission is expired,
all dues are overdue.

The world circles past
muted and gray.
I am an observer,
participant no more.

Perhaps
there may still be time
for some kindred folk
to step on board to join me,

perhaps
some unknown master plan
remains to be evolved,

perhaps
the signal purpose of my life
is yet to be revealed...

The carousel turns.
I wait
with anxiety,
anticipation and
against all reasonable odds,
with hope.

The Mayor and Me

Former mayor of New York Ed Koch
died at the age of 88 in his beloved city.
Son of Polish Jewish immigrants,
feisty and outspoken, his obituary
was on the front page, of course.

The story says he wrote his own epitaph,
paid to have a gravestone carved
and placed in a cemetery of his choice,
in Manhattan naturally. Famously
he always said: How'm I doin'?
Sadly there is no answer to that.

I was born in New York City
of Polish Jewish ancestry
in the very same year.
My resting place is also chosen
though in an adjacent borough.
My obituary will not make the front page,
perhaps a few lines in the local press.

Unlike the mayor my time
has not yet come.
I can still wander the fields of life,
hold out my hand in friendship,
embrace the world with love.

Like the mayor I have tried
to live with truth and passion.
Mr. Mayor, we thank you for your service.
Let it be said as well of me.

Solidarity

Famed folk singer Pete Seeger
died recently at the age of 94.
Bard of our young adulthood,
his death represents the changing
of the guard in protest songs
for social activism.

To my husband of sixty years,
who died one year before at age 87,
it is fitting that you have been joined
by this spirit of our radical youth.

Both of you remained true
to your ideals through ill health
and old age, never ceased
to strum the strings for justice
and equality all over this land,
our land, made for you and me,

never ceased to believe
one man could change the world
one song at a time, one brave
outspoken action at a time.

The torch is passed, rest well.
Together you have earned
your peace in solidarity.

Nonagenarian Musings

I was born in 1924.
The great Israeli poet of the same vintage,
Yehuda Amichai, said it was a good year
to be born. He died in 2000 at the age of 76.
I hope he would approve of me.

Introspection is the hallmark of old age:
what shall I do in my remaining years?
What truths can I realize, what footprints
will I leave upon the sands?

Forgive the cliché, it's time to move on.
In one short decade I will be 100.
Shall we make a date for dinner?
Which restaurant should we go to?

Pick me up at 7:00.
Don't be late.

Beacon in the Night

They call you my loved one
in all the pamphlets they send me
from the hospice team: generic phrase
to describe our sixty years together.
They speak of stages of grief,
the need to acknowledge and accept,
to seek help and consolation.

Do they know the great sadness
that descends in early morning
or quiet of night, not only
for the empty chair positioned
before the TV screen exactly
where you liked it, but sadness
for the human condition,
the necessary brevity of love?

Outside my window a plump robin
stands alert, symbol of the nascent spring
struggling to emerge from winter's grip.
I will take comfort from the chain of life,
each brief existence added to the whole.

Thus have we humans ever breathed,
looked up at the skies and cried:
Here I am, my fragile flame still glows,
a beacon in the night for those to come.

Maturity

It is possible I have stumbled
inadvertently and unaware
upon my longed-for island
of tranquility and peace.

In my mind's eye
through my open window
a virtual green meadow
dotted with flowers unfolds
in all directions to the foothills
of the mountains rising beyond.

It is my choice now
and mine alone
which mountain I shall choose
to scale, which hill to challenge,
which destiny to follow to its end.

Time flows as a river quiet
in maturity, neither turbulent
with rapids nor swollen with flood.

My hand on the tiller,
my face to the sun,
my back to the wind,
I steer my small craft slowly
toward the unknown portal
open to the eternal sea.

To My Husband of 60 Years

You died.
Somewhere in the universe
a master switch was pulled
to shutter your light forever.
I am left to wait my turn,
no one to watch my back.

No one for me to ask:
who ran against Eisenhower in '52?
What was the name of that restaurant
in Juneau that served fiddlesticks,
or the Native American sculptor in Santa Fe
whose work we loved so much?

Was it the Little Big Horn battlefield
in Montana where we bought our silver rings,
or the one in Idaho where Chief Joseph
made his last brave stand?

No one to answer my call, I'm home,
with, what took you so long?

The tether, invisible yet powerful,
has snapped, the door, so firmly closed,
slips open, one push will swing it wide.

Will I find the courage to step through
and face a world newly born,
newly drawn, newly etched
without you?

Legacy

This is what I thought I wanted
through the years of caring for you
tethered to your welfare
tuned to your ever changing needs,
wishing for a time of solitary selfhood
far from the clamor of human frailty,

this day when you have at last released me
to sit on a chaise at the pool
appropriately named Tranquility
at a luxury resort wrested
from the California desert
away from routine and the vagaries
of Connecticut weather

but never far from memories of you
engraved behind my eyes,
imprinted on my DNA,
now longing for the vanished days
of sharing this with you.

Tranquility is a place
not easily arrived at,
an ever-receding goal reached
only through the valley of the self.

Courage has many faces.
My task now is to take
the gift of your life
and move it to the new beginning,
your legacy to me.

Free Will

When I was a child I belonged
to my parents to be molded
in traditions of their forebears.
Even my adolescent rebellion
followed the shape of the mold.

I married a man of appropriate
race, religion and class,
for decades living the scheduled life.
True to my woman's role
I was nurturer and caregiver
for our children, for our parents,
for our cultural institutions,
and finally for my husband
in his sad protracted farewell.

Many times in those busy years
I longed to seek my freedom:
climb aboard a bus, boat or plane
and disappear into the human void.
The ties were tight and strong
of history, custom, family and clan,
and yes, of love.

And now the ties are loosened,
suddenly the door slips open
beckoning with possibilities.
What will it take to step through,
lift my face to sunlight
and say to the universe,
well, here I am, at last!

Renewal

Since you died
I realize I am old:
not that I was not aware before,
but eerily the winds
grow stronger at my back,
cold settles through the roof,
the road ahead climbs steeper
to infinity waiting at the bend.

The mystery of where you've gone
still fills my waking dreams,
your place at the table haunted
by your image, your crooked smile
hovers overhead. Quiet emptiness
slows movement as glaciers poised
at the summit prepare to fill the valleys.

But hold! Summon the wind turbines,
fire up the fossil fuels and nuclear
reactors, bring back the summer solstice
for renewal! I must content myself
to set the memories tenderly aside
and let the earth resume
its natural circuit for whatever time
there is remaining yet to me.

Momentum

When I reached my 80th birthday
a decade ago and more
shock waves spread in all directions.

Years of swimming against
the current toughen the mind and spirit
for those straining toward
an ever-receding shore.

But to live in one's ninetieth year
invokes another dimension:
approaching the event horizon
of a black hole. Time changes
as the inevitable disaster looms.

Would that I could sit on Olympic heights
and embrace the world so soon
to be relinquished!

I would hold my consciousness tightly
to my chest, all senses heightened,
alert for new knowledge, new music,
new feelings, and against
all cosmic odds, new hope.

From The Far Country

My arms are too short now
to embrace the world.

Tissues from an unlucky pig
line my artery walls, an implanted
device provides the current
to pump blood in my heart.
My knees lack cartilage, bone
on bone says the cheerful surgeon.
The physical therapist sent by
a thoughtful government prods
and stretches with weights and bands.

Nevertheless, requiring my attention
is the plane exploded over the Egyptian
desert and the terrorist attacks in Paris.
Desperate refugees seeking sanctuary
are massing at the gates.
When the rising seas overtake
the deltas on which the millions live,
who will take them in?
Where will they go?

My arms are too short now
to embrace the world,
my heart too fragile,
my knees too delicate
to carry me to the barricades.
Only my words remain.

From the far country I summon them:
they are not compromised,
they have no limits,
they can still encircle the globe,
send forth the call for human rights
and dignity, justice with compassion,
universal liberty and truth.

For My 90th Birthday

Why do I feel I have no time?
Indeed, the time I have is infinite.

It reaches to the dome of sky,
to the rim of the solar system
expanding outward with the stars,
unfettered, unencumbered.

I am alone and free in the universe,
no moons encircle me.
I live in my own small sphere,
the atmosphere is mine to breathe.

I am a rogue star
with no set path to follow.
I wander through the cosmos,
no force corrals me to an orbit.

It takes some getting used to,
this sense of separateness
after a lifetime of connection
in the center of the herd.

Perhaps this is the time
to plant my fig tree.

Indeed
the time is now.

About the Author

June Sidran Mandelkern was born in 1924 in Brooklyn, N.Y. She attended local schools including two years at Brooklyn College. In 1968 she earned a BA degree at Hunter College of the City University of New York, and in 1996 an MS degree in Geoscience at Montclair State University in New Jersey. Her husband of sixty years, Robert Mandelkern, a World War II veteran, died in 2013. She has three sons and five grandchildren.

She began writing poetry seriously after moving to Connecticut in 2001, joining the Faxon Poets in West Hartford. Her first book, "Reflections", was published in 2009. She lives and works in West Hartford, CT.

jsmandelkern@gmail.com

36266116R00052

Made in the USA
Middletown, DE
28 October 2016